THE RACE TO SPACE

Clive Gifford
Illustrated by Paul Daviz

words & pictures

Quarto is the authority on a wide range of topics.

Quarto educates, entertains and enriches the lives of our readers—enthusiasts and lovers of hands-on living.

www.quartoknows.com

© 2019 Quarto Publishing plc
First published in 2019 by words & pictures,
an imprint of The Quarto Group.
6 Orchard Road, Suite 100
Lake Forest, CA 92630
T: +1 949 380 7510
F: +1 949 380 7575
www.QuartoKnows.com

A CIP record for this book is available from the Library of Congress.

ISBN: 978 1 78603 890 6

Manufactured in China TT032019

9 8 7 6 5 4 3 2 1

Editor: Harriet Stone
Designer: Kevin Knight
Art Director: Susi Martin
Editorial Director: Laura Knowles
Creative Director: Malena Stojic
Publisher: Maxime Boucknooghe

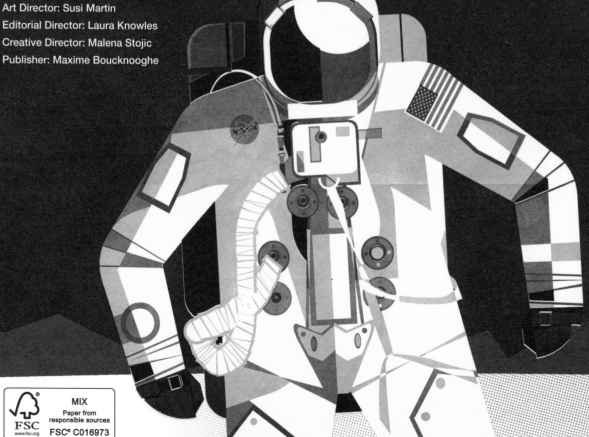

Contents

LOOK UP AND DREAM

Rocket history

For thousands of years, people looked up at the night sky and wondered what it was like, out there in space. But serious, scientific attempts at space travel only began in the 20th century —a period of incredible progress and change. In 1900, no one had ever flown in an aircraft, watched a television, or listened to a radio. Only a few people had even ridden in a car. Yet within 70 years, humans had left Earth to explore space for the first time, and a tiny handful had made it all the way to the Moon. How did this revolution happen?

EARLY ROCKETS

The first rockets were invented in China over 800 years ago. They used gunpowder packed into tubes of bamboo. In the 1920s and 1930s, pioneers like Robert Goddard built the first rockets to burn liquid fuel. These were puny and flew only a few yards high. It took the hard work of thousands of scientists and engineers during the Space Race to turn these early, feeble rockets into massive machines powerful enough to carry astronauts into space.

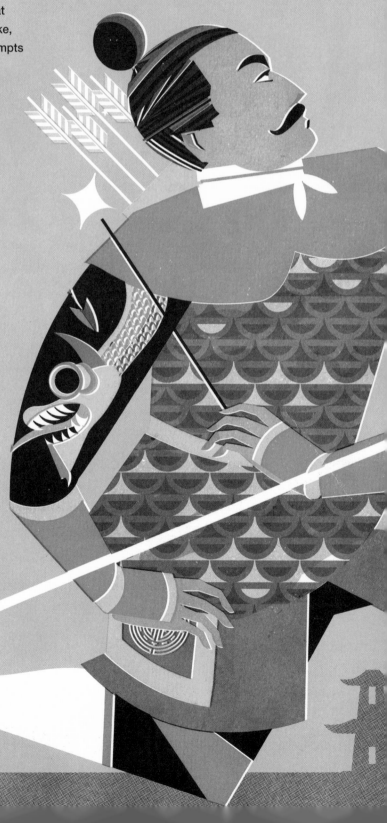

ROCKET ROBERT

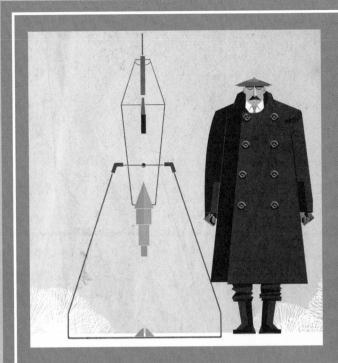

Robert Goddard (1882-1945) pioneered many of the technologies and theories required for sending rockets into space. Many thought his ideas were far-fetched, but Goddard persisted and built gunpowder rockets as well as developing key theories for rocket flight. In 1926, he launched the first ever rocket powered by liquid fuel. It landed in his aunt's cabbage patch but paved the way for future rocket science.

> "The dream of yesterday is the hope of today and the reality of tomorrow."
>
> ROBERT GODDARD

WEAPONS OF WAR

During World War II, Germany produced the terrifying, rocket-powered, V-2 guided missile. It took just minutes to travel hundreds of miles, soaring up to the edge of space, and then plummeting down toward its target. Some of these rockets, and the scientists who made them, fell into the hands of the Soviet and US military at the end of World War II. The US smuggled dozens of V-2 engineers and scientists out of Europe and into the United States.

ROCKET RIVALS

A race to be the first into space began in the 1950s between the two most powerful nations at the time—the United States and the Soviet Union. The rivalry was far from friendly and the competition was intense. Both sides used knowledge gathered during World War II to power their own space programs. This book tells the story of this rivalry and the brave voyages of discovery made by astronauts and cosmonauts as both sides battled for supremacy in space.

SUPERPOWERS COLLIDE

US and Soviets struggle for control

When World War II ended, in 1945, the United States and Soviet Union found themselves the world's two most powerful nations. They fought on the same side during the war, but it had been an uneasy alliance. The two nations had very different views on how to run a country. The Soviet Union was communist, with just one political party and with the state in control of all industries. It wanted to spread communism across the globe, and after the war it introduced communist governments in other countries, particularly in Eastern Europe. Alarmed at this, the United States formed a military alliance with countries in western Europe, called NATO. The USA also offered help to countries or groups who were standing up against communism. The Soviet Union formed its own communist alliance (the Warsaw Pact), and Europe found itself divided in two.

"An iron curtain has descended across the continent."

BRITISH POLITICIAN
WINSTON CHURCHILL, 1946

COLD WAR

A period of tension, hostility, and competition between the superpowers followed. This conflict is now known as the Cold War. It was labeled "cold" as the two sides never declared physical war on each other. Instead, both sides tried to influence events in other parts of the world. This often meant sending troops, weapons, or aid to a particular side in a regional war. They also competed in other ways, such as building large spy networks for gaining secret information, and starting a massive arms race to see who could build the deadliest weapons.

NUCLEAR POWER

The United States was the first country to develop nuclear weapons, and they detonated two devastating atomic bombs in Japan, bringing about the end of World War II. But the Soviets were not far behind. In 1949, they tested their own atomic bomb. With each superpower fearing the other, both built up frighteningly large stores of nuclear weapons. One of the main goals of each country was to find out how to fire these weapons over long distances. To achieve this, they turned to rocket experts for help.

7

ROCKET MEN

Thousands of engineers and scientists in the Soviet Union and the United States worked on missiles during the 1940s and '50s. Each side tried to make them travel faster, farther, and more accurately. Two of these engineers would become world-famous, not as missile makers, but for pioneering the peaceful exploration of space. These gifted rocket men were Wernher von Braun in the USA and Sergei Korolev in the Soviet Union.

SERGEI PAVLOVICH KOROLEV

Born in Ukraine in 1907, young Sergei became hooked on flying at the age of six, when he saw an aerobatics pilot perform spins and tricks. Sergei soon learned to fly gliders and started designing his own aircraft at the age of 17. When he began studying at a technical school in Moscow, Russia, one of his teachers was the great plane designer Sergei Tupolev.

By 1933, Korolev was the chief designer of a group of young rocket engineers known as GIRD. He led the team to launch the country's first liquid-fueled rocket. It only traveled 260 feet (80 meters) into the air, but it was enough to start dreaming about space travel. The country's military became interested and Korolev was offered a job at the Jet Propulsion Research Institute.

The late 1930s was a dangerous time in the Soviet Union. Its leader, Joseph Stalin, had thousands of Soviet politicians, generals, scientists, and engineers tortured and imprisoned. Korolev was one of the victims. He was sentenced to death, then forced to work at a brutal prison camp called a gulag. Korolev suffered beatings and nearly died, before being ordered to return to work on rockets. He wasn't freed until 1944, but after World War II ended, he was put in charge of OKB-1—a Soviet team tasked with building long-range rocket weapons.

"Soviet rockets must conquer space!"

SERGEI KOROLEV, 1933

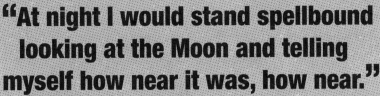

> ## "At night I would stand spellbound looking at the Moon and telling myself how near it was, how near."

WERNHER VON BRAUN, REMEMBERING HIS CHILDHOOD

WERNHER VON BRAUN

Wernher Magnus Maximilian Freiherr von Braun was born in 1912 in an area of Germany that is now part of Poland. As a child, he was fascinated by two things: speed and astronomy. As a teenager, he caused mayhem in the city of Berlin by attaching six enormous fireworks to a toy wagon and firing it down a busy street.

When he was 14, von Braun bought a copy of *The Rocket into Interplanetary Space* by Hermann Oberth, but was disappointed to find that he didn't understand it. Determined to learn advanced math and physics, he studied hard and joined the Society for Space Travel in Berlin. There, he got to meet his hero, Oberth, and the pair even built a small rocket together.

During the war, von Braun worked for the German military at a top secret site in northern Germany. There, he and his staff developed the V-2 rocket that was used in the later stages of World War II. In 1945, von Braun and many of his team surrendered to American troops. Within months, they were living and working at a US Army test site in New Mexico.

Von Braun was soon working on American rocket-powered missiles such as Redstone and Jupiter. However, he remained passionate about peaceful space travel. Throughout the 1950s, he wrote many articles and appeared on television to promote his vision of humans living in space stations and reaching the Moon.

THE COLD WAR HOTS UP

Mega-missile to launch satellite

Throughout the 1950s, the USA and the Soviet Union each built bigger and more powerful rocket engines, so that their nuclear missiles could travel farther. Both Korolev and von Braun found themselves working on destructive weapons when their real passion was peaceful space exploration.

SATELLITE SURPRISE
The International Geophysical Year (IGY), planned for 1957 and 1958, would see over 60 nations work together on science experiments to learn more about the Earth. In 1955, US President Dwight Eisenhower announced that the US would launch a peaceful,

scientific satellite to travel in space during the IGY. The Soviets responded that they, too, would launch a satellite. It would take a huge amount of work to create engines powerful enough to send an object into orbit.

R-7 SEMYORKA

Height: **92–112 feet (28–34 meters)**
Diameter: **9.9 feet (3.02 meters),**
          33.8 feet (10.3 meters) at base
Weight: **309 tons (280 metric tonnes)**
Missile Range: **5,470 miles (8,800 kilometers)**
Fuel: **Kerosene**
Payload: **Up to 12,125 pounds (5,500 kilograms)**

MONSTER MISSILES

Korolev was hard at work on his R series of missiles. One of them, the R-7, was the world's first intercontinental ballistic missile (ICBM), designed to travel thousands of miles between continents. The R-7's first stage lifted the whole machine off the ground before separating and falling away. Then the second stage's engines took over, pushing the missile higher and farther. Although it was a terrifying weapon of war, Korolev had also designed it with another purpose in mind. It would be the perfect satellite launcher…providing it flew.

On August 21, 1957, as he stood at the launch site in Baikonur, Korolev was feeling the pressure. Five launch attempts of his monster R-7 Semyorka had already been called off or ended in disaster. This time, in front of a line of generals, it could not fail. With a deafening roar, all 20 rocket chambers ignited and the 112-foot (34-meter) missile rose from the ground. To the delight of Korolev and the generals, the R-7 traveled over 3,730 miles (6,000 kilometers) .

There was a second successful launch the following month. By the time the USA successfully launched its first ICBM in December 1957, a third R-7 had succeeded in launching the first satellite into space: Sputnik.

SPUTNIK SOARS INTO SPACE

Soviet satellite circles Earth

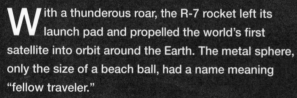

"Listen now for the sound that forever more separates the old from the new."

NBC RADIO ANNOUNCER IN THE UNITED STATES
INTRODUCING SPUTNIK'S BLEEPS TO THE LISTÉNERS

With a thunderous roar, the R-7 rocket left its launch pad and propelled the world's first satellite into orbit around the Earth. The metal sphere, only the size of a beach ball, had a name meaning "fellow traveler."

Korolev's team had worked feverishly to produce Sputnik in the weeks before the launch. The 23-inch (58-centimeter) wide satellite had a metal casing made in two halves held together by 36 bolts. Inside, a ring of heavy batteries weighing 112.4 pounds (51 kilograms) formed a doughnut shape with a small radio transmitter in the hole in the middle. The batteries managed to power the radio for three weeks after launch and Sputnik orbited Earth for a total of three months, a sign that the Space Age had truly begun.

GLEAMING GLORY

Sputnik raced through space at 18,000 miles (29,000 kilometers) per hour, 20 times faster than the speed of sound. It orbited Earth once every 96 minutes, as its four long antennae sent out radio signals. These chirping bleeps could be picked up on radios by people all over the planet. The polished satellite shone brightly and could be spotted glinting in the night sky. The fact that people could see and hear Sputnik, as well as read about it in newspapers, increased its impact and made it headline news. The Soviets were overjoyed with the world's response. It showed them as a technologically advanced nation —the first to launch a working machine into space.

NO NAME, NO NOBEL

Despite his triumph, Korolev's identity remained a secret. A Nobel Prize was offered if the Soviets named the brains behind Sputnik. Soviet leader Nikita Khrushchev refused, declaring that the entire Soviet people deserved the prize. In truth, he thought that singling out Korolev would cause problems within the teams that worked on the program. To the outside world, Korolev remained the mysterious "Chief Designer."

bleep
bleep
bleep
bleep
bleep

"Don't forget this is the Earth's satellite… the very first one. It must also be beautiful."

SERGEI KOROLEV, SPEAKING
TO HIS STAFF ABOUT SPUTNIK

KAPUTNIK!

America's response falls short

Stunned by the success of Sputnik, the Americans sped up their own plans to launch a satellite. In December 1957, the US Navy's Vanguard TV3 rocket launch was broadcast on live television. Unfortunately, it proved an embarrassing and explosive flop. The rocket blew up in a spectacular ball of flames two seconds after liftoff. The newspapers responded with headlines such as "Flopnik," "Oopsnik," and "Kaputnik."

EXPLORER 1 SUCCEEDS
Wernher von Braun had not been involved in the Vanguard mission, but he now got his chance. His Juno rocket, developed from the Redstone missiles, launched the USA's first satellite, Explorer 1, on January 31, 1958.

Explorer 1 was long, thin, and only one-sixth of the weight of Sputnik, but its body was crammed with scientific sensors. These detected tiny space particles called micrometeoroids that struck the satellite, as well as areas of radiation surrounding the Earth. These regions were named the Van Allen Belts and were the first major discovery made in space. Explorer 1's batteries ran out in May 1958, but it kept orbiting Earth until 1970.

SPACE SUSPICIONS

Space was now in the news and many Americans were excited at the thought of space travel and exploration. However, others were fearful of Soviet machines like Sputnik flying over the United States many times a day. In 1958, after the successful launch of Sputnik 3, Soviet leader Nikita Khrushchev boasted about his country's superiority in space technology and knowledge. The USA became determined to close the gap.

"America sleeps under a Soviet moon."

NIKITA KHRUSHCHEV, 1958

1957

December 6

The US government set up new schemes, such as increasing science lessons in schools, and created new organizations. Some of them, such as ARPA, were dedicated to military space research, while the National Aeronautic and Space Administration (NASA) focused on peaceful space exploration. In 1959, 5,000 staff were moved from the US Department of Defense to NASA and its budget for the year 1960 was tripled. America meant business!

SPACE ZOO

Animal astronauts blast off

The Soviets had little time to enjoy Sputnik's success, as Sputnik 2 was scheduled to launch just over a month later. Korolev had promised Khrushchev that this next mission would carry a living creature. The ultimate goal was to send humans into orbit, but the effects of space travel on life were unknown, so animals were sent first.

FROM THE STREETS TO SPACE

Sputnik 2 carried a stray dog found on the streets of Moscow, named Laika. The capsule also had oxygen supplies, medical sensors, and a TV camera which beamed back images as she became the first living thing to orbit Earth. People around the globe were stunned by the ambitious mission. The Soviets, however, kept a secret: Laika had died from the heat just a few hours into the mission.

ASTRO ARK

In August 1960, a test mission of the Soviets' new Vostok spacecraft carried a pair of rats, two dogs named Belka and Strelka, 42 mice, a gray rabbit, flies, and a number of plants. It orbited Earth for 26 hours, and this time there was a happy ending: all the creatures returned safely to Earth. This proved that the spacecraft's life-support systems could work for a human passenger. When Strelka had a litter of puppies the following year, Khrushchev sent one, called Pushinka, to the US president, John F. Kennedy. After being thoroughly checked for hidden spy microphones, she lived happily at the White House.

SPACE CHIMP!

Although Laika performed the first full Earth orbit, she was not actually the first living creature in space. The US military used V-2 rockets to launch fruit flies in 1947 and a monkey in 1949. Twelve years later, a chimpanzee named Ham flew in a Mercury capsule, just three months before the first American astronaut. Ham had been trained to pull levers when lights flashed to receive banana pieces as a reward. He demonstrated that work could be done in space by performing the same task during his mission. When he returned safely to Earth, suffering only a bruised nose, he became a celebrity.

ASTRONAUTS WANTED

Space traveler training begins

After the animals, it was time for humans in space. Both sides started selecting candidates in 1959. Early spacecraft were small, so astronauts needed to be small as well. The USA only selected candidates under 6 feet (1.81 meters) tall, less than 181 pounds (82 kilograms) and under the age of 40. Soviet cosmonauts had to be less than 5 feet, 7 inches (1.7 meters) tall and under the age of 30.

THE FIRST ASTRONAUTS

NASA's first astronauts were all military test pilots, as these men were used to high speed and massive G-forces from their work testing fast jet aircraft. More than 500 test pilots applied. After lots of tests and medical examinations they were whittled down, first to 110 applicants, then to 32, then finally the Mercury Seven were introduced to the world in April 1959. The Soviets also selected pilots as their 20 cosmonaut candidates, half a dozen of whom were chosen as contenders for the first mission and known as the Vanguard Six.

TOUGH TRAINING

All trainee astronauts underwent long periods of intense training. They were drilled hard for peak physical fitness and constantly tested to see if they could stay calm and perform under pressure. They had to study hard—taking courses on astronomy, medicine, physics, mechanics, and rocketry, as well as learning how every part of their spacecraft worked.

As part of their training, the Mercury Seven —along with a replica of their spacecraft—were dumped in the Nevada desert for four days, to practice their survival skills. The Soviet cosmonauts also endured tough survival training that involved roasting in superheated saunas before plunging into icy water. Each cosmonaut also made around 50 parachute jumps, on land and in water.

WANTED
SPACE PIONEERS

Must be smart, short-ish, young, brave, and prepared to push yourself to the limit…and beyond.
Jet fighter pilot qualification required.

PREPARING FOR SPACE

Some of the training tried to mimic the likely effects of the conditions in space. Cosmonauts spent 10–15 days alone in an isolation chamber, while NASA astronauts spent hours in dark, soundproof water tanks. The NASA recruits also took rides in aircraft that climbed and dived sharply to produce short spells of weightlessness. Astronauts sometimes felt sick on these training flights, which became known as "vomit comets."

Further tough trials awaited astronauts on the ground. Complicated machines whizzed the trainees around to mimic the extreme gravity, known as G-force, they could expect during space travel. One US machine known as "the wheel" was particularly despised, with astronauts calling it "a gruesome merry-go-round." Astronauts were strapped inside a ball on a long arm and spun at over 125 miles (200 kilometers) per hour. As a result they experienced 8–15 times the gravity felt on Earth and found it hard to see or breathe.

1959

WOMEN IN SPACE

In 1960–61, 13 American women between the ages of 23 and 41 were trained and tested in similar ways to the Mercury Seven. They performed well but were not selected for spaceflights. The Soviets added five women to its cosmonaut team in 1963, while the first American female astronaut, Sally Ride, wouldn't reach space until 1983.

"15G was our limit on the wheel and it was no fun at all."

APOLLO 11 ASTRONAUT
MICHAEL COLLINS

ONE WILD RIDE

In one training activity, Mercury astronauts were strapped into a seat inside three aluminum cages. Powered by nitrogen jet thrusters, each cage moved the astronaut in a different direction with dizzying speed—up to 30 spins a minute. This ultimate rollercoaster ride, called MASTIF or the gimbal rig, simulated tumbling out of control in space. Disorienting and terrifying, the astronauts had to use hand controls to right themselves. It was a challenging test.

"It was one of the more demanding training exercises ...we grew to hate that gimbal rig, passionately."

JOHN GLENN,
MERCURY ASTRONAUT

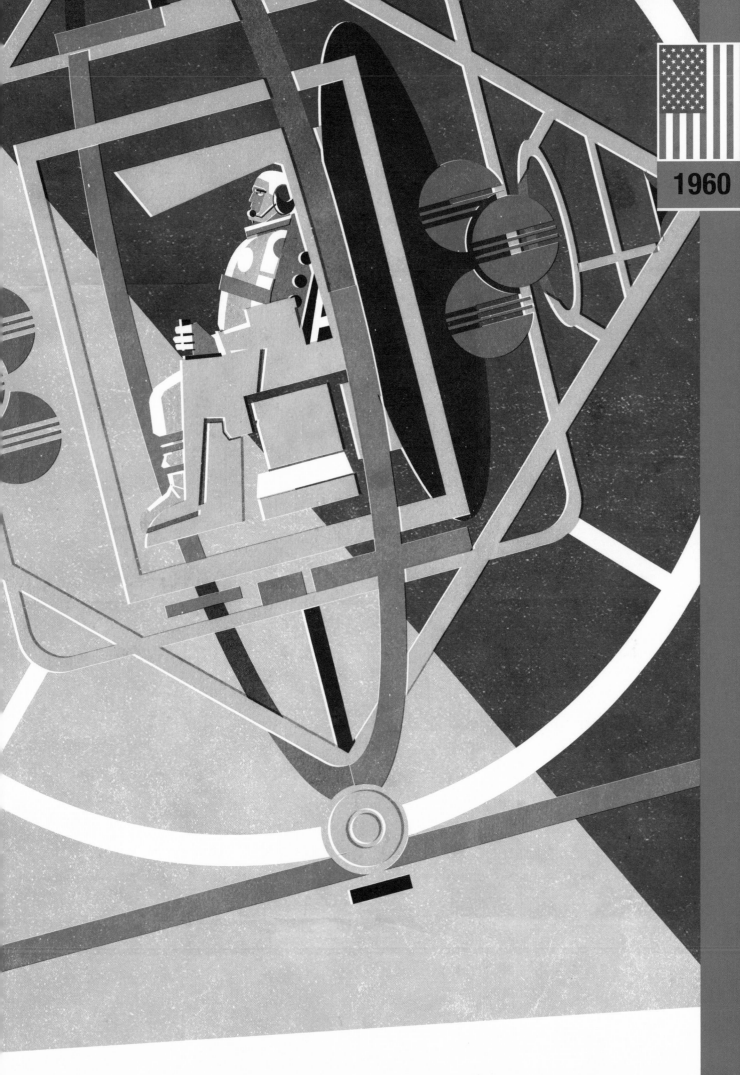

"Don't be afraid, I am a Soviet like you, who has descended from space."

YURI GAGARIN

FIRST MAN IN SPACE

Soviet officer orbits Earth

" Poyekhali!"—"Off we go!" shouted Yuri Gagarin above the roar of Vostok-K's rocket engines. As a teenager, he'd worked as a steelmaking apprentice, a dock laborer, and, for almost two years during World War II, he had lived in a tiny mud hut after German forces took over his home. Now he was lying on his back inside a 7.5-foot (2.3-meter) -wide steel ball called the descent module, about to become the first person in history to head into space.

Gagarin had only qualified as a pilot in 1957 but during cosmonaut training he was the popular choice to be the first Soviet in space. His fitness, intelligence, and calmness under pressure made him stand out, as did his size; Gagarin was just 5 feet, 2 inches (1.57 meters) tall—handy, as the spacecraft was smaller than a phone booth! But Gagarin didn't know he was about to make history until just three days before liftoff.

The days before the launch were incredibly tense for Chief Designer, Sergei Korolev. The Vostok program had tens of thousands of workers, 120 organizations, and 36 factories. Everything had to be just right for the voyage into the unknown, and even then there were fears about how space flight would affect the human body. Vostok had no rescue plan or backup engines. If something went drastically wrong and Gagarin got marooned in space, all he had was ten days of food rations.

THE LAUNCH

The rocket was launched at 9:07 a.m. Moscow time. After just 118 seconds of hurtling skyward, the Vostok-K's rocket boosters were used up and fell away. They were followed shortly after by the main rocket, leaving the spacecraft to cruise into orbit above Earth. Gagarin caught glimpses of his wild ride through three portholes. He marveled at the weightlessness of space, watching his pencil drift out of his grasp and a drop of water float in midair.

It wasn't long before the Vostok's engines fired, to begin re-entry and bring Gagarin back to Earth. The instrument module and descent module were supposed to separate before re-entry, but this did not go quite as planned, and the spacecraft began spinning wildly. Inside, Gagarin experienced G-forces eight times those on Earth—but he didn't panic. He even whistled "The Motherland Hears, The Motherland Knows," a patriotic Soviet song in which the second line is: "Where her son flies in the sky."

At 23,000 feet (7,000 meters) above the ground, Gagarin's ejection seat fired, his parachutes opened, and he spent 10 minutes floating toward the ground. His sudden landing back on Earth alarmed some local farmers but he calmly explained, "Don't be afraid, I am a Soviet like you, who has descended from space…and I must find a telephone to call Moscow!"

A SPACE LEGACY

Gagarin's trip into space had only lasted 108 minutes, but its effects were felt worldwide. The Soviets spread news of their triumph and allowed Gagarin to travel abroad where he was greeted as a celebrity. He was now too valuable, as a mark of the Soviets' achievement, to be risked in space again, so Gagarin returned to train future cosmonauts.

THE ROUTE

①Launch, ②In orbit, ③Vostok 1 passes into darkness above the Pacific Ocean, ④Vostok 1 emerges into daylight above the Atlantic Ocean, ⑤Retro-rocket fire for re-entry, ⑥Vostok 1 re-enters Earth's atmosphere, ⑦Gagarin lands back on Earth's surface

PLAYING CATCH-UP

American astronauts reach space

It didn't take long for the US to respond to the Soviets' success. Less than four weeks after Gagarin's mission, US astronaut Alan Shepard was launched into space in a Mercury craft he named Freedom 7. The US had been making careful preparations, carrying out 17 test launches before Shepard was blasted from Cape Canaveral in Florida.

Shepard's mission lasted only 15 minutes and 22 seconds, much shorter than Gagarin's, but it was groundbreaking in its own way. Freedom 7 was the first spacecraft to be controlled in space by an astronaut. Shepard used levers which fired small rocket thrusters to steer.

QUICK PROGRESS

The next eighteen months were a hectic period in the American space program, with five more Mercury missions launched. One of them nearly ended in disaster. Astronaut Virgil "Gus" Grissom almost drowned in the Atlantic Ocean after his capsule's hatch came off too early, letting water flood in. However, other missions went more smoothly.

In the third Mercury launch, John Glenn became the first American to complete an orbit of the Earth, while in the last Mercury mission Gordon Cooper circled Earth 22 times.

SANDWICH IN SPACE

The next step after the Mercury missions was the Gemini program. This was a scaled-up version of Mercury, with a spacecraft that could carry a crew of two. ("Gemini" means "twins" in Latin.) Its first crewed mission blasted off in 1965, carrying Gus Grissom, John Young, and a surprise corned-beef sandwich! Space food at the time was dried into cubes, sealed in pouches, or squeezed out of tubes like toothpaste. In the weightless conditions in space, floating crumbs could jam the spacecraft's electrical circuits. However, John Young smuggled the sandwich on board in a spacesuit pocket. The mission went smoothly, but he got into trouble afterward due to the unnecessary risk.

MOON TALK

In May 1961, less than three weeks after Shepard's mission, US President John F. Kennedy gave a historic speech. He said, "I believe that this nation should commit itself to achieving the goal, before this decade is out, of landing a man on the Moon and returning him safely to the Earth." Kennedy's speech also warned that no single space project would be more impressive, difficult, or expensive to accomplish.

For the USA, at least, the space race now had a finish line. Millions of dollars were poured into research, staff, and building new machinery and facilities. NASA's budget tripled between 1960 and 1962, then doubled again in 1963. By 1965, an astonishing 4 percent of all the money the American government spent was going to the space agency.

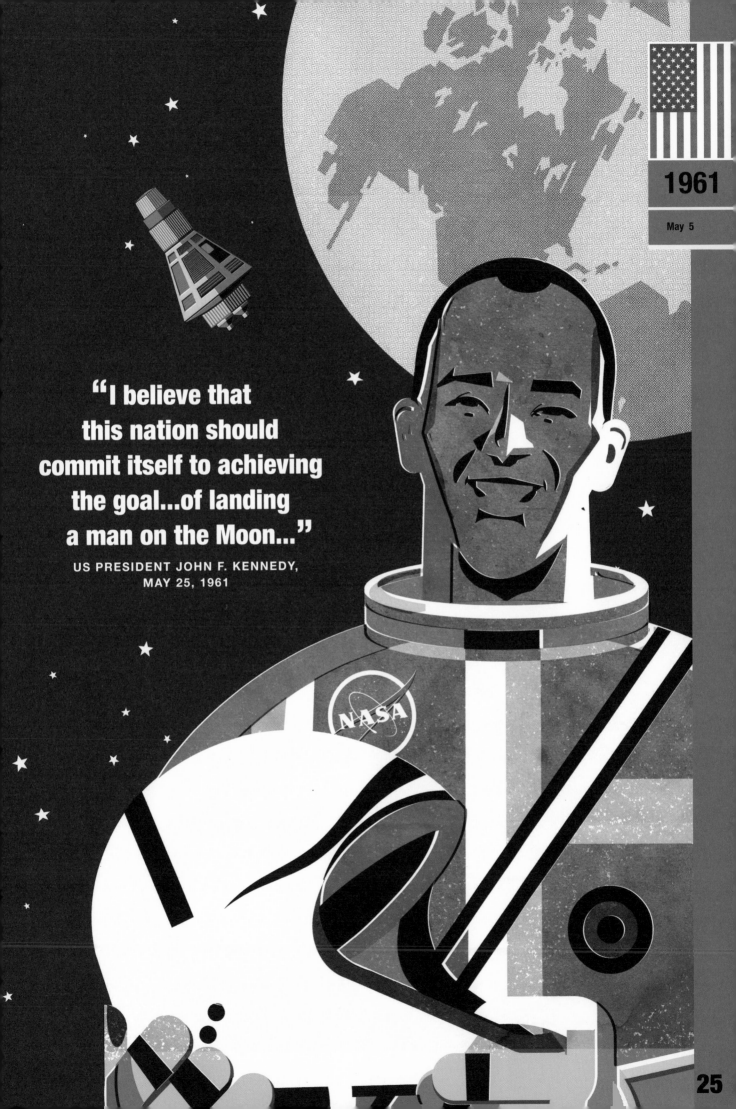

"I believe that this nation should commit itself to achieving the goal...of landing a man on the Moon..."

US PRESIDENT JOHN F. KENNEDY, MAY 25, 1961

1961

May 5

SOVIET STRIDES

Valentina Tereshkova: first woman in space

her record of 126 successful parachute jumps. After 18 months of hard training, she was selected for the Vostok 6 mission and made 48 orbits of Earth. Tereshkova became a Russian hero, but it would be 19 years before another woman flew in space.

ALL CHANGE

In the early 1960s, Sergei Korolev's team were extremely busy. They were planning four more Vostok missions, designing the new Soyuz spacecraft, and were working on Korolev's master plan—a giant N1 rocket, capable of sending humans to the Moon. In February 1964, however, they were ordered to change plans. NASA's two-man Gemini mission would soon launch for the first time and the Soviet leader, Nikita Khrushchev, wanted to upstage it with a Russian spacecraft carrying a crew of three...and quickly!

THREE'S A CROWD

The next Vostok missions were immediately canceled and parts of those spacecraft were used to build a three-man craft called Voskhod, meaning "sunrise." The craft didn't have a lot of room, and the designers had a real headache fitting everything in. Out went the ejection seats and even the cosmonauts' spacesuits. Instead, they wore woollen tracksuits!

Eight months later, Voskhod 1 completed its mission, reaching a record altitude of 209 miles (336 kilometers) above Earth. During their 24 hours and 17 minutes in space, the crew received radio congratulations from Khrushchev. But by the time the cosmonauts arrived back on Earth, the Soviet leader had been removed from power. A mission designed to upstage the Americans' efforts in space had been bumped from the headlines by major political news.

> **"Once you've been in space, you appreciate how small and fragile the Earth is."**
>
> VALENTINA TERESHKOVA

The Soviets were boosted by the success of Gagarin's flight and launched five more Vostok spacecraft. The first, in August 1961, carried 25-year-old Gherman Titov, who made 17 orbits of the Earth in Vostok 2. He still holds the record as the youngest person to fly into space, and also became the first person to sleep in an orbiting craft. Titov claimed that sleeping in space was easy "once you got your arms and legs arranged properly." Vostoks 3 and 4 were launched within a day of each other in August 1962, showing the world that the Soviets were capable of more than one mission at the same time.

WONDER WOMAN

Valentina Tereshkova was a factory worker who enjoyed skydiving in her spare time. Inspired by Gagarin's flight, she volunteered for the Soviet space program in 1962 and was accepted, partly due to

PROBE WARS

Machines boldly go

The competition between the USA and the Soviet Union wasn't just about sending humans into space. Both sides turned to uncrewed machines, known as space probes, to learn more about space and gain an edge over their rival.

Probes can be built smaller and lighter than crewed spacecraft, which require many bulky systems to keep astronauts alive. Probes can also be sent to places too hostile for humans and can go on one-way missions, never to return. In the early days of the space race, both sides had far more failed probe missions than successes. NASA even sent pairs of Mariner probes on identical missions in case one failed.

NASA took close-up photos of the Moon with the Ranger probes in the 1960s and scored big successes with two Mariner space probes. Mariner 2 was the first probe to reach another planet. It flew by Venus in 1962 and measured the planet's surface temperature as a sizzling 800 °F (425 °C). Mariner 4 headed off to Mars two years later. It took 228 days to reach the planet, where it beamed back photos of its surface for the very first time. The Soviets had less success with Mars, but their Venera 4 probe did travel through Venus' atmosphere in 1967 and Venera 7 safely landed on the planet's surface three years later.

TO THE MOON

The USA scored an early partial success in 1958 with Pioneer 4, which got to within 37,280 miles (60,000 kilometers) of the Moon. The following year, the Soviets launched Luna 1, aiming to crash into the Moon—but it missed by 3,670 miles (5,900 kilometers) and whizzed off into space, ending up orbiting the Sun instead. The very next year, Luna 2 was more successful, smashing into the lunar surface at high speed. Luna 3 launched just a few weeks later, stunning the world when it flew around the Moon and took photographs of its far side, which people had never seen before.

SPACEWALK!

Cosmonaut out in space

Standing in a tiny inflatable airlock fixed to the side of the Voskhod 2 spacecraft, Alexey Leonov took a deep breath. Trusting his luck, training, and the Soviet technology, he stepped away from the safety of the spacecraft and out into space. No one had ever performed a spacewalk before. The Soviets had kept the event so secret that not even his family knew what was planned.

THE SILENCE OF SPACE

After the roar of the launch, the whirring machinery, and the radio chatter inside Voskhod 2, Leonov was stunned by the silence he experienced out in space. All he could hear was his beating heart and his labored breathing. Leonov spent 12 minutes and 9 seconds outside the spacecraft, attached to it by a 17.5-foot (5.35-meter) -long tether. His spacesuit kept him alive, supplying oxygen, but it didn't keep him cool. He became drenched in sweat that filled his spacesuit up to his knees. Leonov fixed a camera to the side of Voskhod 2, but couldn't take photos with his chest-mounted camera—his spacesuit had inflated too much. This also meant he couldn't squeeze back inside the airlock. Leonov had to risk everything by letting a dangerous amount of oxygen out of his suit. After a struggle, he threw himself head first into the airlock and rejoined his fellow cosmonaut, Pavel Belyayev.

ROUGH LANDING

The exhausted cosmonauts then discovered that the spacecraft's automatic landing system had failed. They used a backup, but the delay meant they landed hundreds of miles away from their intended landing site on Earth, deep in a freezing Siberian forest. They spent two nights in sub-zero temperatures, hoping to ward off any wolves or wild bears with their shared pistol, before rescuers arrived.

US SPACEWALK

Two and a half months after Leonov's mission in 1965, Ed White performed the first US spacewalk, leaving Gemini 4 to spend 20 minutes in space. The following year, Edwin "Buzz" Aldrin performed three spacewalks totaling more than five hours. These missions proved that astronauts could perform useful work in space.

BUILDING THE SATURN V

America's most complex machine

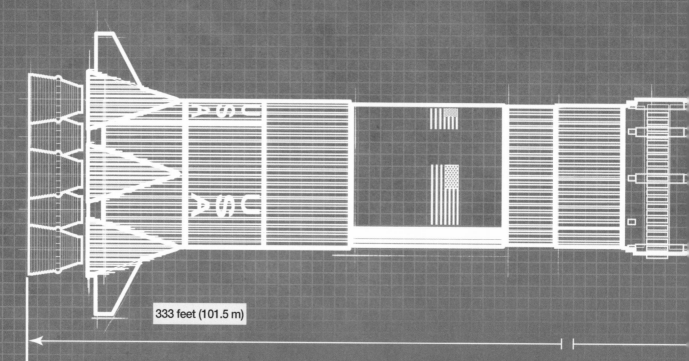

333 feet (101.5 m)

First stage

It would take a huge amount of power to send a heavy spacecraft like Apollo to the Moon—and the Saturn V would provide it. Von Braun and his team worked on the supersized launch vehicle throughout the Mercury and Gemini projects. They had to solve thousands of problems, big and small, along the way.

The massive Saturn V was more than three times the height of the Titan II, which had been used to launch the Gemini spacecraft. It contained over three million parts and its construction involved workers from 20,000 different companies—a great achievement in organization.

BUILT FOR POWER

In total, 13 Saturn V rockets were launched by NASA throughout the 1960s and '70s. Each rocket was made up of three stages. The first stage was by far the most impressive. Turbopumps as powerful as 30 diesel trains fed five F-1 rocket engines. Together, the engines burned 14.3 tons (13 metric tonnes) of fuel and liquid oxygen every second.

The first stage's rockets were designed to fire for less than three minutes, by which time the Saturn V would be 41.6 miles (67 kilometers) above Earth. Then it would fall away and the second stage's five J-2 rocket engines would take over, firing for around six minutes. Finally, the third stage, containing one J-2 engine, would increase the speed of the spacecraft to 25,000 miles (40,000 kilometers) per hour, sending it on its way to the Moon.

APOLLO TAKES SHAPE

Apollo spacecraft would sit on the very top of Saturn V and were created to carry astronauts to the Moon. Like the rocket, it was also very complicated to build. It went through many improvements, including over 600 changes in the winter of 1966 alone. The spacecraft's three separate modules (service, command, and lunar) were designed to cruise together through space to a position within 68 miles (110 kilometers) of the Moon. Only one of the sections, the Lunar Module, would actually descend to the Moon's surface.

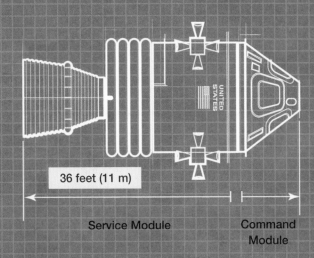

36 feet (11 m)

Service Module

Command Module

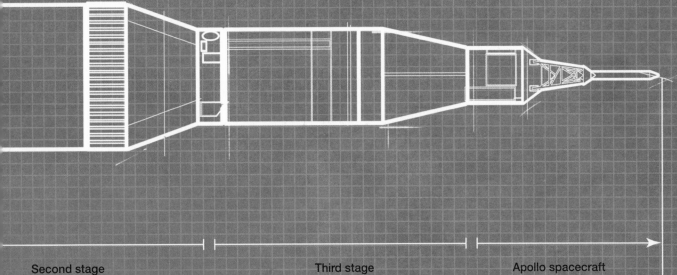

Second stage

Third stage

Apollo spacecraft

MOON LANDING MACHINE

The Lunar Module looked bulky and awkward, but it didn't need to be streamlined as there is no air resistance in space. Fuel would account for two thirds of the module's weight. There would be enough fuel to descend to the lunar surface and then to blast off the Moon for the journey home.

"We called it the Bug."

ASTRONAUT EUGENE CERNAN, SPEAKING ABOUT THE LUNAR MODULE

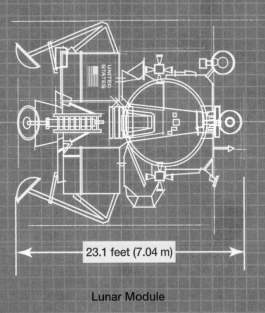

23.1 feet (7.04 m)

Lunar Module

SATURN V

This is Saturn V, the rocket designed by Wernher von Braun, along with tens of thousands of colleagues at NASA, to carry humans to the Moon. No launch vehicle had ever stood so tall (362.5 feet/110.5 meters), weighed so much (6.4 million pounds/2.9 million kilograms), or possessed so much heart-stopping power. It was a truly awe-inspiring sight as this giant machine roared up into the sky on its first test launch from the Kennedy Space Center, in November 1967. A total of 12 Saturn V rockets would be launched during the Apollo program.

"The building is shaking! Look at that rocket go... oh, the roar is terrific!"

TV REPORTER WALTER KRONKITE
AT THE FIRST SATURN V LAUNCH

MODULE MANEUVERS

Apollo's daring design required complex maneuvers in space. The upcoming missions were planned down to the very last detail.

Once away from Earth, the Apollo Command and Service Modules (CSM) would leave the Saturn V, turn around, and then dock with the Lunar Module, which would be released from the rocket by panels that opened like flower petals. The three modules would then cruise together to the Moon, before the Lunar Module undocks and descends to the Moon's surface. On the return journey, the top half of the Lunar Module would blast away from the Moon. Perfect timing would be needed for it to re-dock with the CSM orbiting the Moon, before heading back to Earth. A number of Apollo missions would be launched to rehearse some of these maneuvers before a real Moon landing could be attempted.

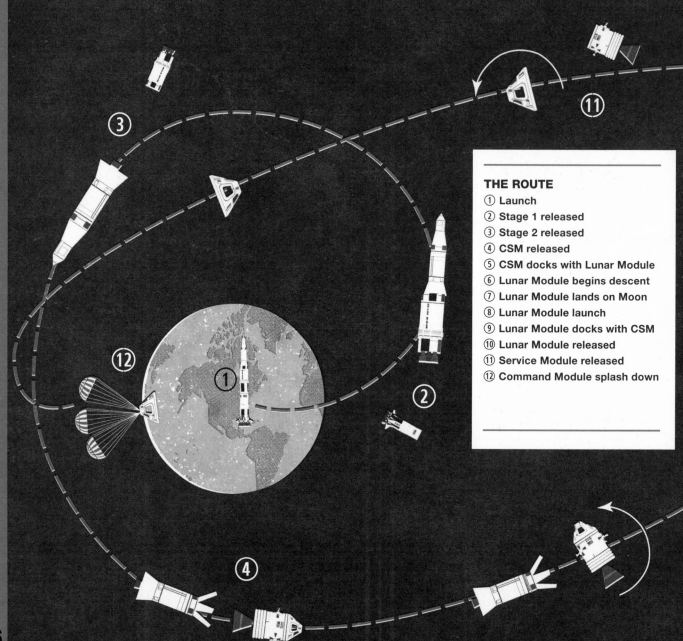

THE ROUTE
1. Launch
2. Stage 1 released
3. Stage 2 released
4. CSM released
5. CSM docks with Lunar Module
6. Lunar Module begins descent
7. Lunar Module lands on Moon
8. Lunar Module launch
9. Lunar Module docks with CSM
10. Lunar Module released
11. Service Module released
12. Command Module splash down

“A cosmonaut will always continue to challenge the universe.”

THE SOVIET COSMONAUT GROUP WRITING IN PRAVDA NEWSPAPER, APRIL 1967

BOUNCING BACK

Agencies cope with tragedy

Making it to the Moon and back carried big risks, and both sides were forced to cope with tragedies and setbacks during the race. In 1966, Sergei Korolev died. Without their chief designer, the Soviet Union struggled to complete their massive N1 rocket necessary to launch cosmonauts to the Moon.

Then in early 1967, both sides suffered tragic deaths among their space forces. A fire inside an Apollo test spacecraft claimed the lives of Gus Grissom, Ed White, and Roger Chaffee, while the first flight of the new Soyuz spacecraft ended in the loss of cosmonaut Vladimir Komarov. Yet the Soviet Union and the United States both pledged to continue. "A cosmonaut will always continue to challenge the universe," vowed Komarov's colleagues. Neither side, however, sent another person into space until October 1968, when the Russian Soyuz 3 and the American Apollo 7 both flew successfully.

UPS AND DOWNS

While investigations into the disasters were carried out and new safety features were designed, progress was made with uncrewed missions. Five out of NASA's seven Surveyor probes landed successfully on the Moon, and in 1968 a Lunar Module was sent into space for the first time. On the ground, Apollo astronauts trained hard using craft called LLRVs (Lunar Landing Research Vehicles). These were odd-looking, jet-powered frames which mimicked how the Apollo Lunar Module would be controlled in space. Luckily, they came equipped with an ejection seat, which once saved Neil Armstrong's life, blasting him away to safety moments before his LLRV crashed in Houston, Texas, in May 1968.

ASTRO-TORTOISE

In 1968, the Soviets launched Zond 5. The spacecraft carried plants, seeds, worms, flies, two tortoises, and a 5 foot, 9 inch (1.75-meter) human dummy packed with sensors to detect harmful radiation. Zond 5 circled the Moon and splashed down safely in the Indian Ocean six days later. Its occupants survived, proving that living things could return safely from the Moon. This success worried the United States—the Soviets seemed close to making it to the Moon. Who would win the race?

ASTRONAUTS OUT OF THIS WORLD

Apollo 8: Christmas in space

NASA decided to take a big risk. Boosted by Apollo 7's success a few months earlier, but worried about the Soviets beating them to the Moon, they took a gamble. The next Apollo mission would be a real test of their spacecraft's abilities. The Lunar Module was not yet ready to carry humans, so instead NASA's ambitious plan was to send three astronauts in Apollo's Command and Service Modules to orbit around the Moon for the first time. The mission would take place over Christmas, launching on December 21, 1968.

The three astronauts were the first to travel on top of the gigantic Saturn V rocket and feel its formidable power as it blasted off the launch pad. Two crew members, mission commander Frank Borman and James A. Lovell, had been into space before, but William Anders was a rookie. In just three minutes the crew were over 56 miles (90 kilometers) above Earth, heading into orbit around the planet. After thorough checks the Saturn V's third stage rocket fired, and Apollo 8 was on its way to the Moon. It reached its target on Christmas Eve.

EARTHRISE

Orbiting as close as 69 miles (111 kilometers) from the Moon, the astronauts took photographs of the gray, cratered lunar surface. They also made six live TV broadcasts during their mission. On the fourth of Apollo 8's ten orbits, the Earth appeared above the lunar landscape. Anders took a photo of the "Earthrise," which soon became world-famous. No one had ever seen that view of Earth before. The planet looked small, delicate, and beautiful, its blue oceans covered in wispy white clouds.

FIRST CHRISTMAS IN SPACE

Christmas Day morning was a tense time at NASA's Mission Control. It was the day that Apollo 8 had to start its 57-hour journey

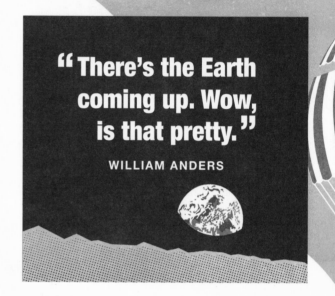

" There's the Earth coming up. Wow, is that pretty. "

WILLIAM ANDERS

back to Earth. The crew made another TV broadcast that afternoon before opening a locker containing their Christmas meal. The food on the mission so far had been freeze-dried and tasteless, but the astronauts found a Christmas surprise—foil pouches wrapped in red and green ribbons and labeled "Merry Christmas." Inside was real turkey, gravy, and cranberry sauce—a Christmas treat enjoyed more than 186,000 miles (300,000 kilometers) from home.

After 147 hours and 42 seconds, and a journey of 579,607 miles (932,787 kilometers), the crew splashed down in the Pacific Ocean, close to the USS *Yorktown* whose divers and helicopters helped them to the ship. Their mission had been a resounding success, capturing the world's imagination, with an estimated one billion people —over a quarter of the global population—viewing it on TV. Even the Soviets acknowledged the triumph, with the chairman of one Soviet space program, Boris Petrov, praising Apollo 8 as "an outstanding achievement of American space sciences and technology."

BORMAN LOVELL ANDERS

NAVY
HS-4
66
2711
NU

THE RACE GAINS PACE

Final preparations for Moon mission

1969 would be a landmark year for both nations and their plans to reach the Moon. It started well for the Soviets in January, when Soyuz 4 and Soyuz 5 became the first vessels to dock in space and transfer crew from one craft to another.

Two months later, the Americans followed suit, docking two spacecraft—Apollo 9's CSM and Lunar Modules—for the first time. It was a resounding success and paved the way for Apollo 10 in May the same year. Apollo 10 was a dress rehearsal for a crewed Moon landing. Inside its Lunar Module, astronauts Thomas Stafford and Eugene Cernan got tantalizingly close to the Moon—less than 9.3 miles (15 kilometers) from the surface.

SOVIET PLANS

The Soviets were planning to send a single cosmonaut to the Moon, but they were still experiencing problems with their N1 launch vehicle. The 56-foot (17-meter) -wide rocket had five stages, compared to Saturn V's three, and a staggering 30 rocket engines in the first stage alone. In addition to all the engines, the rocket had a vast network of pipes, valves, and pumps, and getting all of these to work together perfectly was proving extremely difficult.

The first attempt at an N1 launch occurred in February 1969. It lasted just three minutes and three seconds before the giant machine crashed back to Earth, 32 miles (52 kilometers) away. A second launch attempt occurred in July, which ended with the biggest explosion in the history of space exploration. The rocket rose less than 650 feet (200 meters), fell back onto its launchpad, and blew up. Wreckage was thrown over 6 miles (10 kilometers) away, and it would take 18 months to rebuild the launchpad. Soviet hopes would be further dashed later that month with the launch of NASA's Apollo 11 mission.

NEXT STOP: THE MOON

Apollo 11 blasts off

The alarm rang to wake Michael Collins, Buzz Aldrin, and Neil Armstrong. It was just over five hours before they would start their journey to the Moon on board Apollo 11. The three men had several things in common: they were all born in 1930, weighed 165 pounds (75 kilograms), and had been into space before on a Gemini mission. They had all trained for many years, using simulations of their spacecraft and the Moon's surface.

After a breakfast of steak and eggs, the astronauts' chests were shaved so that medical sensors could be attached. They then got into their heavy spacesuits, carrying small silver suitcases containing an oxygen supply and an air conditioner to keep them cool. At the launch site, they climbed into Apollo 11's Command Module, which was perched on top of an enormous Saturn V. The astronauts would spend more than two hours in place before liftoff as a long list of final checks were made.

THE JOURNEY BEGINS

More than a million people lined the roads bordering the Kennedy Space Center. They watched the Saturn V's engines ignite, sending the giant launch vehicle slowly into the air. The last words the astronauts heard from Launch Control in Florida were, "Good luck and Godspeed." Neil Armstrong replied with thanks and said, "We know this will be a good flight." Within 12 minutes, Apollo 11 was over 100 miles (160 kilometers) above Earth.

Following an uneventful cruise through space, Apollo 11 began orbiting the Moon on July 19th. The following day, after thorough tests of all systems, Armstrong and Aldrin crawled through the short, narrow tunnel that linked the CSM and the Lunar Module. The crew had named their Lunar Module *Eagle*, after the United States' national bird. Once inside, they detached and *Eagle* began its descent to the surface.

PROBLEMS ARISE

Communications were lost on several occasions during the descent and Mission Control in Houston, Texas, were close to calling the mission off. The Apollo Guidance Computer was primitive by today's standards, with one million times less memory than a modern smartphone. It flashed several warning codes, which alarmed the astronauts. A bigger worry, however, was discovering that *Eagle* was not on target as it got within 650 feet (200 meters) of the surface. Instead of the smooth, level ground they had expected, below them lay an area strewn with craters and huge boulders.

Armstrong took control of the Lunar Module for the last part of the descent, relying on his experience and training to fly to a more suitable landing site within a flat plain called the Sea of Tranquility. He needed to be quick, as fuel was desperately low. Aldrin helped by checking on all the instruments and calling out altitude and other crucial information. Mission Control signaled that there was 60 seconds of fuel left. Then they were down to 30 seconds, and *Eagle* still wasn't on the ground. But moments later, the long probes on *Eagle's* legs registered contact with the lunar surface. After a short pause, Armstrong's voice crackled over the radio, "Houston, Tranquility Base here…The Eagle has landed." Mission Control erupted in celebration. Humans had finally reached the surface of the Moon.

"The Eagle has landed."

NEIL ARMSTRONG

1969

July 20

ONE SMALL STEP

Armstrong makes history

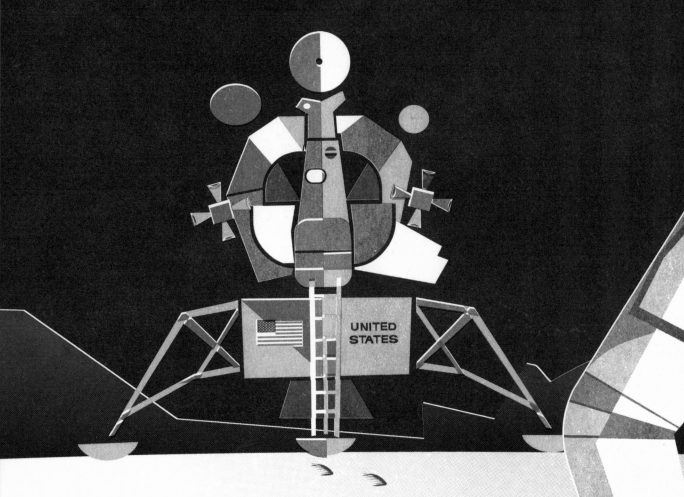

UNITED
STATES

N eil Armstrong felt his way down the short
ladder that took him to the lunar surface.
His bulky spacesuit meant he couldn't see his feet.
Although he and Buzz Aldrin were supposed to
rest for five hours after landing, they had chosen
instead to stay up and prepare. As his feet touched the
surface, Armstrong uttered the words, "That's one small
step for a man, one giant leap for mankind." These words
and Armstrong's steps were watched live, in amazement,
by 600 million people—almost a sixth of the world's
population at the time.

"Nothing prepared me for the starkness of the moon.

BUZZ ALDRIN

1969

July 21

47

COMING HOME

Apollo 11 returns to Earth

Neil Armstrong would spend 2 ½ hours on the Moon's surface with Buzz Aldrin joining him for most of that time. The pair traveled up to 230 feet (70 meters) from their spacecraft, setting up experiments, gathering moon rocks, planting a US flag, and leaving medals to honor Soviet cosmonauts who had died during the Space Race. While the world marveled at the television images, Armstrong and Aldrin headed back inside the Lunar Module for a well-earned rest. Armstrong curled up on the ascent engine's cover while Aldrin lay sprawled on the floor—both still in their bulky spacesuits. Meanwhile, Michael Collins, orbiting in Apollo 11's CSM, and Mission Control on Earth were both fretting about what many considered the most perilous part of the mission—getting the two astronauts off the Moon.

Disaster nearly struck when Armstrong and Aldrin discovered that the switch which helped fire the Lunar Module's engine had broken off. Aldrin stuck a metal pen into the hole to solve the problem, and soon the top half of the Lunar Module had liftoff. Seven minutes later they were in orbit around the Moon and four hours later their module docked successfully with the CSM, reuniting them with Michael Collins.

SPLASHDOWN!

The Apollo 11's command module capsule was traveling at over 15,500 miles (25,000 kilometers) per hour when it entered the Earth's atmosphere. As it streaked through the sky, the outside of the capsule heated up to over 4,350 °F (2,400 °C) and the heat shield melted away. The atmosphere acted like a brake on the spacecraft and three large parachutes further slowed its fall, before the capsule splashed down in the Pacific Ocean.

A helicopter airlifted the astronauts to the nearby aircraft carrier USS *Hornet*, where the three men entered a converted caravan trailer called the Mobile Quarantine Facility. At the time, NASA was worried that the astronauts might bring back unknown harmful substances or diseases from the Moon, so the Apollo 11 crew were isolated from the world as they traveled back to the United States. The astronauts stayed in quarantine until August 10th. Three days later they set off to take part in parades through New York, Chicago, and Los Angeles, cheered on by huge crowds.

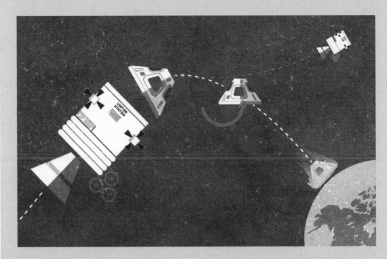

FINAL SEPARATION

Just over 194 hours after liftoff, Apollo 11 performed its final undocking maneuver. The Command Module, holding the three astronauts, separated from the Service Module. While the Command Module headed toward Earth, the Service Module was destroyed, burning up in Earth's atmosphere.

MACHINES ON THE MOON

1970

November 17

Soviet probes land successfully

Three days before Apollo 11 left Earth, the Soviets launched a last attempt to beat the Americans to the Moon. They weren't ready to send a cosmonaut into space. Instead the daring uncrewed Luna 15 mission was designed to collect a sample of Moon rock and return it to Earth ahead of Apollo 11.

NASA was worried that the two missions would clash, but the Soviet Union released details of their flight plan. Problems with the probe kept it in orbit for days, while in the meantime Armstrong and Aldrin arrived on the Moon. The astronauts were still exploring the surface when Luna 15 crashed into the Sea of Crises—an area just north of Apollo 11. The Soviets tried again the following year with Luna 16. It collected 3.56 ounces (101 grams) of lunar soil and rock fragments which were successfully brought back to Earth. In 1993, three specks of this Moon material, weighing just 0.2 grams, were sold at auction for $442,500!

MOON ROVER

The Soviets' next mission to the Moon was a large remote-controlled rover called Lunokhod. In 1970 it rumbled more than 6 miles (10 kilometers) across the Moon's surface, examining rocks and features with its scientific instruments. The rover was designed to operate for only two months, but it ended up working for 321 days and beamed back over 20,000 black-and-white photos to Earth. While it didn't grab many headlines, it was a major technical achievement.

SPACE SALVAGE

By the time Lunokhod landed on the Moon, NASA had launched two more Apollo missions, Apollo 12 and Apollo 13. Apollo 12 carried Pete Conrad and Alan Bean to the lunar surface. They landed just 600 feet (183 meters) away from the Surveyor 3 space probe, which had been sent by NASA to investigate the Moon two years earlier. The probe was examined, and its TV camera and other parts were brought back to Earth by the astronauts.

"HOUSTON, WE'VE HAD A PROBLEM..."

Apollo 13 fight for survival

NASA had been successful with its first attempt at landing humans on the Moon, so further Apollo missions continued as planned. Aldrin and Armstrong's stay on the Moon had been short and there was so much more to explore and learn about.

NASA's next endeavor was Apollo 13. Apart from one engine shutting down a little early, the first two days of the mission progressed smoothly. So smoothly, in fact, that 46 hours into the flight, mission controller Joe Kerwin told the three astronauts, Jim Lovell, Fred Haise, and Jack Swigert, "The spacecraft is in real good shape as far as we are concerned. We're bored to tears down here." He wouldn't be bored for long.

DISASTER STRIKES

Fifty-six hours after liftoff, the crew felt a jolt and heard a bang as warning lights flashed ominously on the craft's display. An oxygen tank had exploded, damaging the Service Module and the second oxygen tank, which soon emptied. It was only later in the mission that Jim Lovell saw the damage and exclaimed, "There's one whole side of that spacecraft missing."

Without oxygen from the tanks, the fuel cells that supplied the spacecraft with electricity and drinking water failed. Landing on the Moon was no longer an option. The goal now was survival, but the astronauts were a long, long way from home.

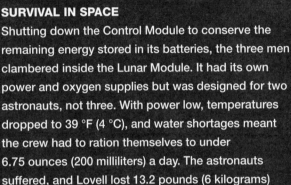

SEARCHING FOR A SOLUTION

Feverish calculations were made in space and on the ground. Mission Control came up with various plans to get the astronauts back. A simple U-turn using the Service Module engine was too risky, so the Lunar Module's engine was fired to send the craft on an orbit around the Moon, swinging it back toward Earth. At one point, the astronauts were 248,655 miles (400,171 kilometers) from Earth—the farthest any human has ever been from the planet. Flying this vast distance using just the Lunar Module engine, which was designed for much shorter trips, would be a real challenge.

SURVIVAL IN SPACE

Shutting down the Control Module to conserve the remaining energy stored in its batteries, the three men clambered inside the Lunar Module. It had its own power and oxygen supplies but was designed for two astronauts, not three. With power low, temperatures dropped to 39 °F (4 °C), and water shortages meant the crew had to ration themselves to under 6.75 ounces (200 milliliters) a day. The astronauts suffered, and Lovell lost 13.2 pounds (6 kilograms) in weight.

On the ground, preparations were being made for their return. The Soviet Union put aside its rivalry and sent ships to likely splashdown areas on Earth. They also switched off radio transmitters that might interfere with signals to and from the stricken spacecraft.

After three days of nerve-shredding tension and planning, Apollo 13 was ready to enter its final phase. The three astronauts powered up the Command Module, climbed inside, and began their descent through the Earth's atmosphere. Millions of people who had followed the unfolding drama on TV hoped and prayed all would go well. On April 17th the astronauts splashed down safely in the Pacific Ocean and were given a hero's welcome. The mission is remembered, in the words of Jim Lovell, as "a successful failure."

1970

April 14

"There's one whole side of that spacecraft missing!"

LAST MAN ON THE MOON

Apollo 17 heads home

Eugene Cernan paused as he took his last steps on the Moon. He and Harrison Schmitt had spent over 22 hours outside on the very last Apollo lunar mission, Apollo 17. The pair had roamed 22.4 miles (36 kilometers) and collected 146 pounds (66 kilograms) of rock and soil samples. As Cernan returned to the Lunar Module, he etched the initials of his daughter, Tracy, into the dusty lunar surface. As the Moon has no winds or water, those initials and Cernan's footprints remain there to this day.

SUCCESSFUL MISSIONS

Apollo 17 was the last of four successful Apollo missions that followed Apollo 13. The last three of these made use of an ingenious Lunar Roving Vehicle (LRV), folded up and stored in the bottom half of the Lunar Module. Electric motors drove the rover's four steel wheels, allowing astronauts to explore greater distances than on foot.

Many experiments were performed in space and on the lunar surface during these missions. Devices measured the Moon's thin atmosphere and probed below the surface for any moonquakes. Apollo 14 tested whether tree seeds could survive space. Most germinated into healthy saplings, which were later planted around the United States and farther afield. The Apollo missions returned a total of 842 pounds (382 kilograms) of Moon rocks, some of which were 3.2 billion years old.

> " We leave as we came and, God willing, as we shall return, with peace and hope for all mankind. "

EUGENE CERNAN

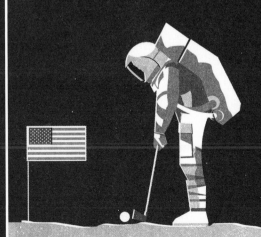

SPORT IN SPACE

One unauthorized experiment involved Alan Shepard, the first American in space, who smuggled golf balls and a club onto Apollo 14. Shepard's bulky spacesuit restricted his golf swing and his first attempt flew off into a crater. But his second soared away and, in the Moon's weak gravity, traveled hundreds of yards. The golf balls, three Lunar Roving Vehicles, and many other pieces of equipment are still on the Moon, along with a plaque left by the departing Apollo 17 crew. Its first sentence reads: "Here Man completed his first exploration of the Moon."

HANDSHAKE ACROSS SPACE

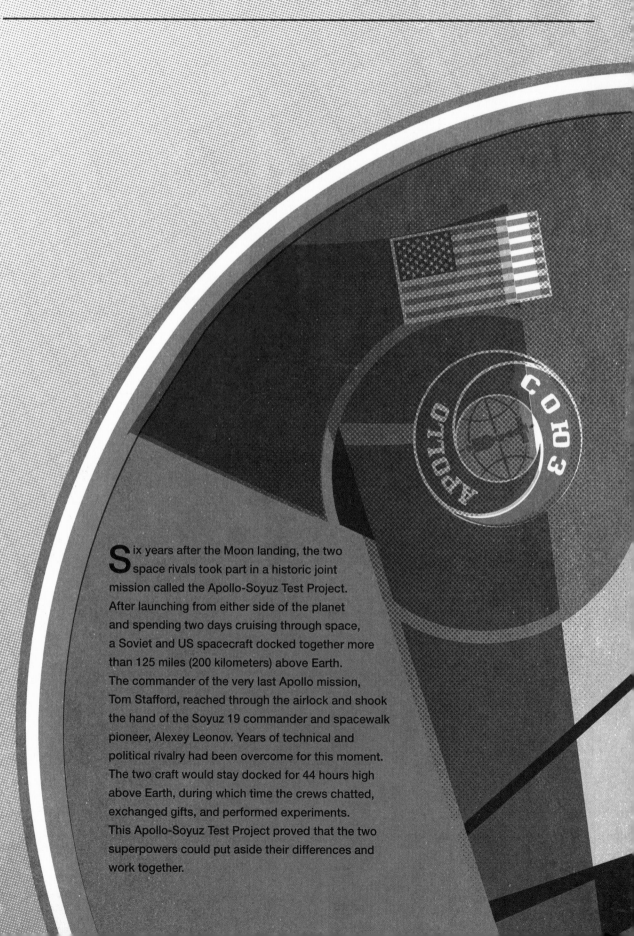

Six years after the Moon landing, the two space rivals took part in a historic joint mission called the Apollo-Soyuz Test Project. After launching from either side of the planet and spending two days cruising through space, a Soviet and US spacecraft docked together more than 125 miles (200 kilometers) above Earth. The commander of the very last Apollo mission, Tom Stafford, reached through the airlock and shook the hand of the Soyuz 19 commander and spacewalk pioneer, Alexey Leonov. Years of technical and political rivalry had been overcome for this moment. The two craft would stay docked for 44 hours high above Earth, during which time the crews chatted, exchanged gifts, and performed experiments. This Apollo-Soyuz Test Project proved that the two superpowers could put aside their differences and work together.

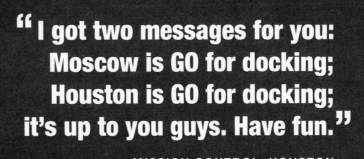

WORKING TOGETHER

Superpowers cooperate

Although the competition of the Space Race ended in the 1970s, space exploration continued. NASA sent probes to moons, planets, and asteroids, landed roving robots on Mars, and built a fleet of reusable space planes—the Space Shuttle. The Soviets gave up on crewed Moon missions after further failures of their N1 rocket. Instead, they concentrated on Soyuz missions and the building of space stations. In 1986, they launched the Mir space station. It was built block-by-block in space and was expected to last five years, but orbited Earth for fifteen years.

A NEW ERA

At the end of 1991, the Soviet Union split into Russia and 14 smaller, independent nations. Russia and the US agreed to collaborate in space and NASA's fleet of Space Shuttles made 11 flights to Mir, as both sides shared knowledge and equipment. In 1994 Sergei Krikalev became the first cosmonaut to travel on a Space Shuttle, and the following year

Norman Thagard became the first American to ride a Soyuz craft into space.

Both sides worked together on other missions as well. NASA's Jerry Linenger made a five-hour spacewalk in a Russian Orlan spacesuit, while Shannon Lucid spent 179 days living on Mir. At the time, this was the longest period spent in space by any woman and any American.

THE ISS OPENS

In 1998, the first parts of the most ambitious space project ever blasted into Earth's orbit. A Russian module called Zarya was followed by a US module called Unity, and another Russian module, Zvezda. These were assembled in space to form the start of the International Space Station (ISS), which first welcomed astronauts on board in 2000. Russia and the USA were joined in this project by other nations, including Japan, Canada, and the European Space Agency. But it is the two space superpowers who run the ISS from mission controls based in Houston, Texas, and Moscow, Russia.

THE END OF THE RACE

The Space Race made important contributions besides teaching us about the Solar System. It advanced many areas of science and inspired thousands of people to become scientists and engineers. It also led to crucial new technologies being invented or their development speeded up—from robots and computer microchips to space satellites that monitor Earth, help forecast the weather, and beam TV and phone signals around the planet.

> **"We rely on each other literally for our lives, so despite any...past history, we get along just great."**
>
> NASA ASTRONAUT MARK KELLY

LIVING IN SPACE

More than 230 astronauts from 18 different nations have visited the ISS so far. They live and work in space often for six months at a time, in an area the size of a six-bedroom house—a far cry from the cramped capsules of the early space race. Since 2011, when NASA's Space Shuttles retired, all astronauts travel to and from the ISS in Soyuz spacecraft, all launched from the Baikonur Cosmodrome in Kazakhstan where, in 1961, Yuri Gagarin blasted off into history.

INTERNATIONAL SPACE STATION

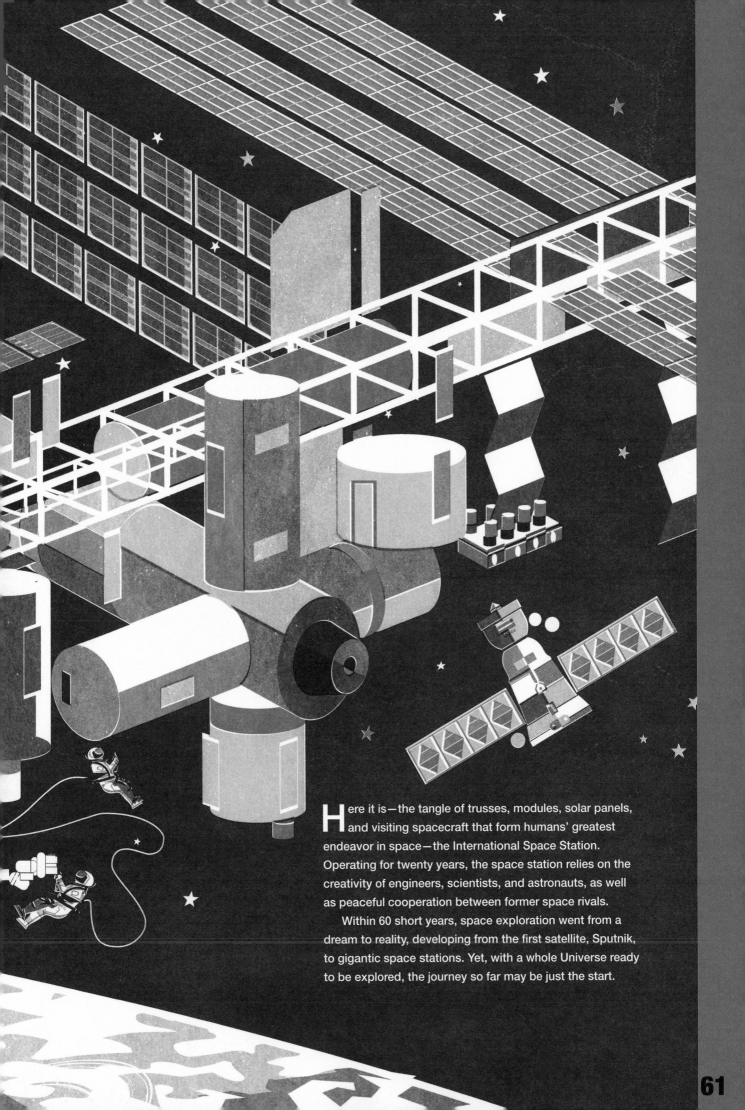

Here it is—the tangle of trusses, modules, solar panels, and visiting spacecraft that form humans' greatest endeavor in space—the International Space Station. Operating for twenty years, the space station relies on the creativity of engineers, scientists, and astronauts, as well as peaceful cooperation between former space rivals.

Within 60 short years, space exploration went from a dream to reality, developing from the first satellite, Sputnik, to gigantic space stations. Yet, with a whole Universe ready to be explored, the journey so far may be just the start.

SPACE INVENTIONS

The space race sparked a boom in science and technology as vast amounts of research were carried out and many new objects and materials were developed. Some entered everyday life and proved very useful—from freeze dried foods and cordless power tools to memory foam, which was first developed to give test pilots and astronauts more comfortable seating, but is now used in shoes, seats, and crash helmets.

INSULATION INVENTION

Insulating materials protected spacecraft and probes from the extreme temperatures in space. The development of this led to two valuable inventions. Thin foil space blankets are now used to warm up people suffering from the cold, while a sandwich made of two layers of foil with a plastic center is commonly used to insulate homes.

COMPUTER BOOST

The space race gave a big boost to computer technology, leading to smaller, faster machines that run using powerful chips called microprocessors. NASA also pioneered the use of joysticks as controllers and developed computer chips used as digital cameras for its probes to take photos in space. Similar chips are now used in smartphones worldwide.

MEDICAL MATTERS

Space race breakthroughs have led to specialized medical equipment, such as heart pumps which are based on the pumps of rocket engines, and invisible braces for your teeth made from see-through ceramics. A coating used to toughen up astronauts' visors is now used on scratch-resistant lenses for eyeglasses.

FINDING YOUR WAY

Satellites developed during the space race now relay millions of phone calls, TV, radio, and internet signals around the world every day. Groups of satellites such as the US GPS (Global Positioning System) and the Russian GLONASS system provide pinpoint navigation for smartphones and other similar devices.

POPULARIZED PRODUCTS

NASA and other space agencies didn't invent solar panels, Velcro, or Teflon, but by using them in their spacecraft, they helped make them more popular.

TIMELINE

1926
American engineer Robert Goddard launches the first liquid-fueled rocket.

1942
First test flight of rocket-powered V-2 missile. It is launched as a weapon two years later.

1945
Wernher von Braun moves from Germany to the United States to work on US missiles.

1957 August
The first ICBM, an R-7 from the Soviet Union, is successfully launched.

1957 October
Sputnik becomes the first artificial satellite in space.

1958
The National Aeronautics and Space Administration (NASA) is formed.

1959
The United States and the Soviet Union select their first astronauts and cosmonauts.

1959 October
The Soviet probe Luna 3 takes pictures of the far side of the Moon for the first time.

1961 April
Yuri Gagarin becomes the first person in space, aboard Vostok 1.

1961 May
Alan Shepard, in a Mercury spacecraft, becomes the first US astronaut in space.

1962
Mariner 2 reaches Venus, becoming the first probe to reach another planet.

1963
Vostok 6 takes Valentina Tereshkova into orbit, making her the first woman in space.

1965 March
Alexei Leonov becomes the first person to perform a spacewalk.

1966 January
Sergei Korolev, chief designer on the Soviet Union's space program, dies.

1967
The Saturn V rocket is launched for the first time in a test mission called Apollo 4.

1968 October
An Apollo spacecraft carrying three astronauts makes its first successful spaceflight.

1968 December
Apollo 8 completes the first crewed orbit of the Moon.

1969 July
Apollo 11 performs its historic mission, landing Neil Armstrong and Buzz Aldrin on the Moon.

1970
The Lunokhod rover becomes the first machine to travel across the Moon's surface.

1970 April
Apollo 13 nearly ends in disaster after an oxygen tank explodes.

1971
Apollo 15 astronauts use the Lunar Roving Vehicle for the first time.

1972
Apollo 17 carries the last humans to walk on the Moon, Eugene Cernan and Harrison Schmitt.

1975
An Apollo and a Soyuz spacecraft dock in space as part of the first international space mission.

1981
The first flight of NASA's Space Shuttle—the first reusable spacecraft—takes place.

1983
Sally Ride, flying in a Space Shuttle, becomes the first American woman in space.

1986
The first modules of the Mir space station are launched. Mir orbited Earth until 2001.

1998
The first module of the International Space Station (ISS) is launched into space.

2017
After her third ISS mission, Peggy Whitson holds the record for the most time spent in space by an American or a woman, totaling 665 days.

2019
Three lunar rovers, from Germany, the United States, and India, will be launched to the Moon, as well as a Russian lander called Luna 25.

2020
NASA's Mars 2020 rover will launch in July.

INDEX

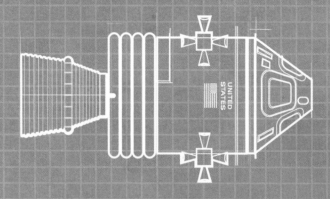